Fourth Position Finger Exercises for the Cello

by Cassia Harvey

CHP229

©2013 by C. Harvey Publications All Rights Reserved.
6403 N. 6th Street
Philadelphia, PA 19126
www.charveypublications.com

Fourth Position Finger Exercises for Cello

Cassia Harvey

2

Fourth Position Finger Exercises for the Cello

Fourth Position Finger Exercises for the Cello

7

CHP229 ©2013 C.Harvey Publications All Rights Reserved.   www.charveypublications.com

8

Fourth Position Finger Exercises for the Cello

CHP229 ©2013 C.Harvey Publications All Rights Reserved.

www.charveypublications.com

10

Fourth Position Finger Exercises for the Cello

Fourth Position Finger Exercises for the Cello

11

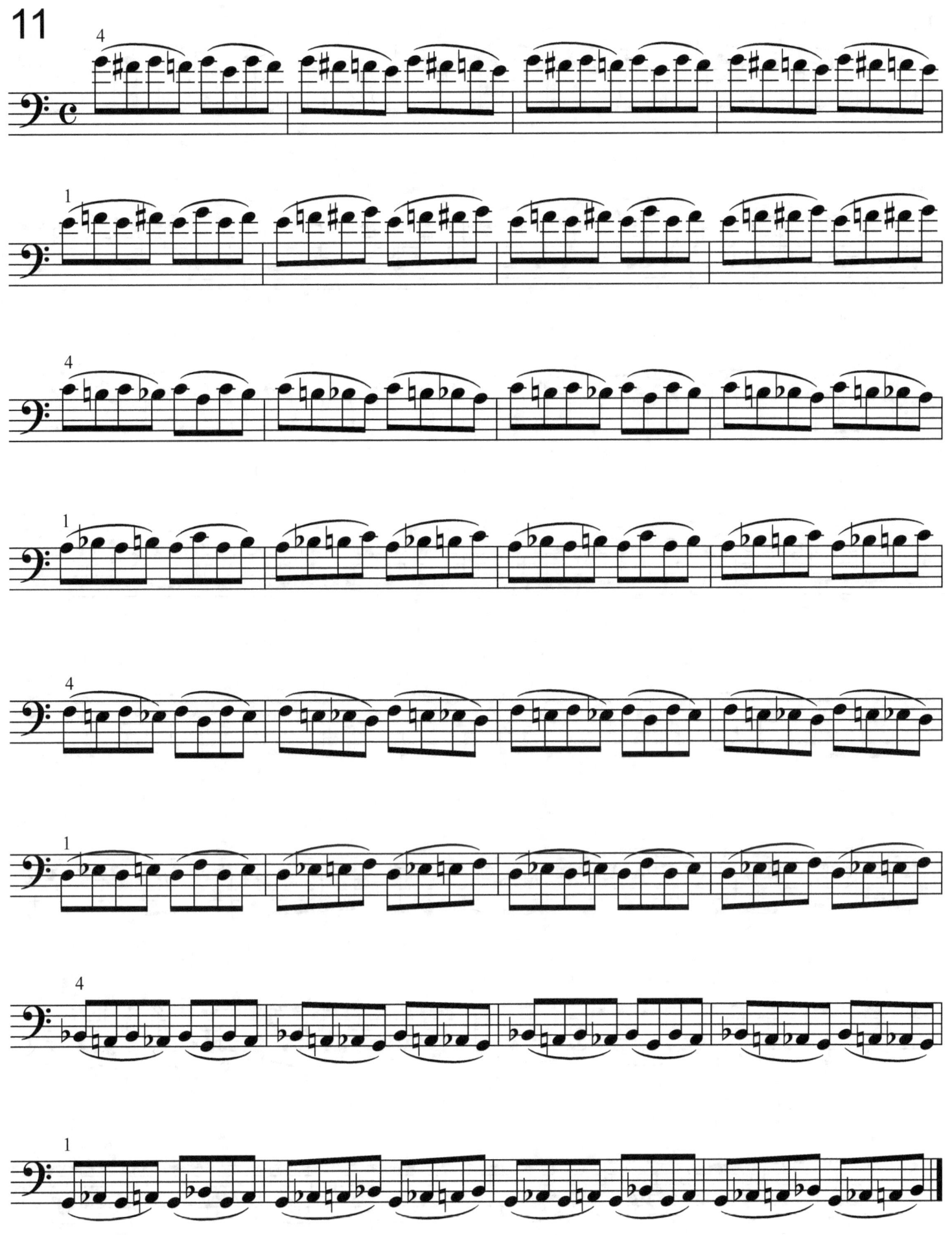

12

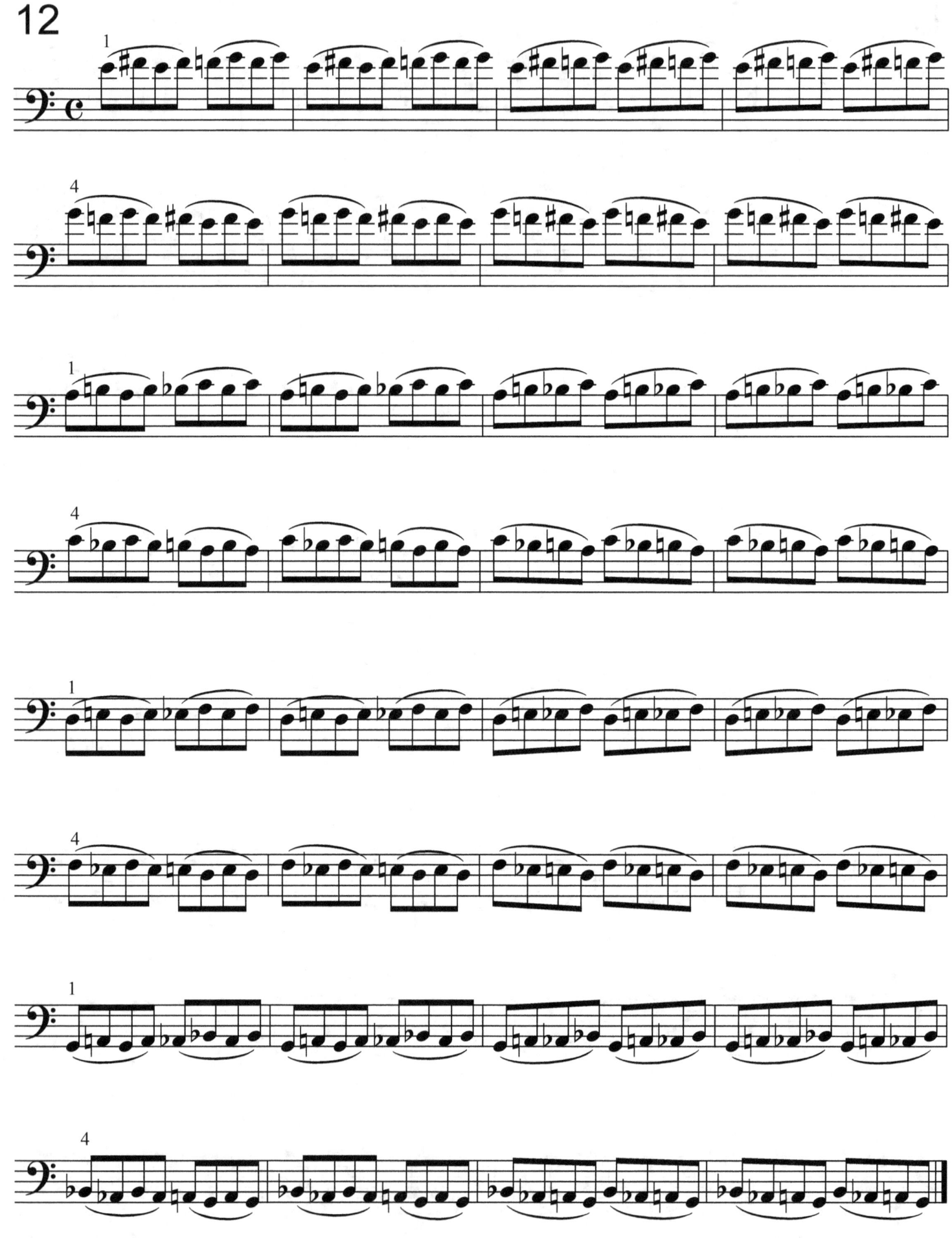

Fourth Position Finger Exercises for the Cello

CHP229 ©2013 C.Harvey Publications All Rights Reserved.

14

Fourth Position Finger Exercises for the Cello

Fourth Position Finger Exercises for the Cello

15

16

Fourth Position Finger Exercises for the Cello

Fourth Position Finger Exercises for the Cello

17

18

Fourth Position Finger Exercises for the Cello

20

Fourth Position Finger Exercises for the Cello

22

Fourth Position Finger Exercises for the Cello

23

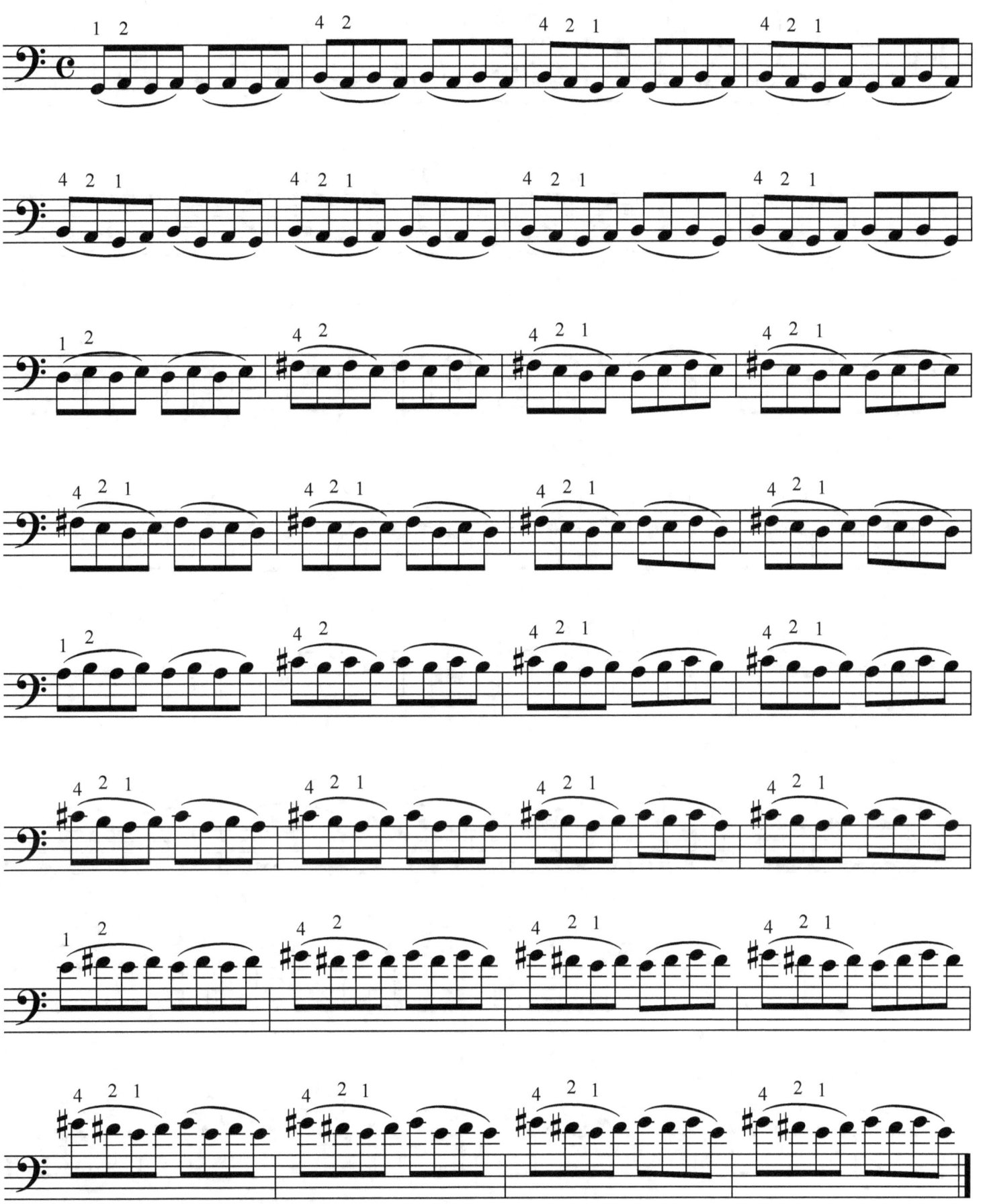

24

Fourth Position Finger Exercises for the Cello

25

available from www.charveypublications.com: CHP243
Cello Stretching: Extended First Position

Part One: Stretching Back to a Flat

Cassia Harvey

In closed first position, the space between first and second fingers is a half step:

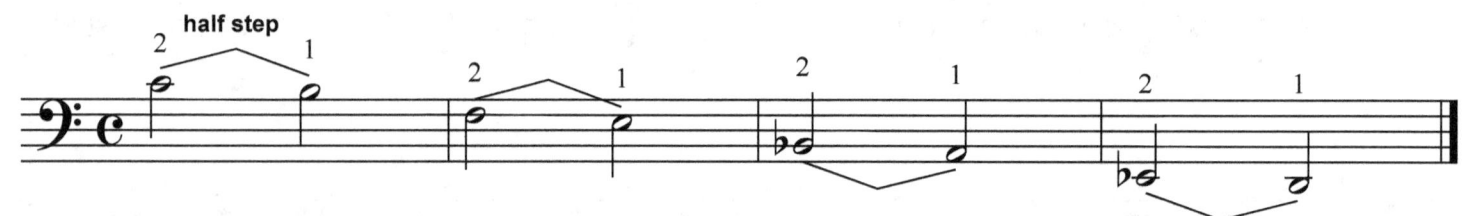

In order to reach some flats, the first finger extends back, while the other fingers remain in first position:

The 2nd, 3rd, and 4th fingers are in closed (regular) first position

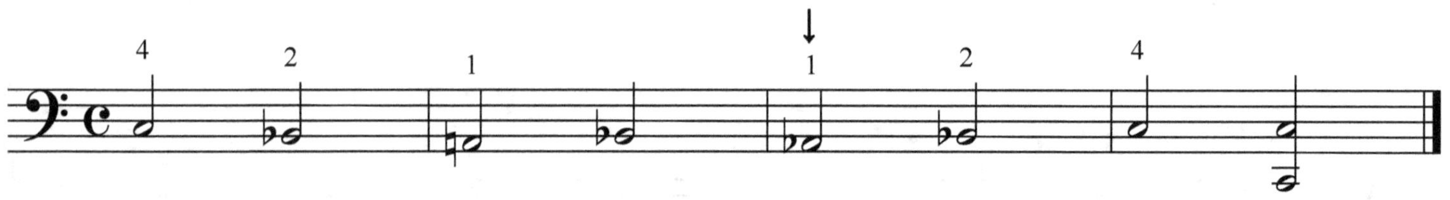

©2014 C. Harvey Publications All Rights Reserved.